Forces

Angela Royston

raintree

a Capstone company — publishers for children

Raintree is an imprint of Capstone Global Library Limited, a company incorporated in England and Wales having its registered office at 264 Banbury Road, Oxford OX2 7DY – Registered company number: 6695582

www.raintree.co.uk
myorders@raintree.co.uk

Edited by Linda Staniford
Designed by Steve Mead
Picture research by Kelly Garvin
Production by Victoria Fitzgerald
Originated by Capstone Global Library Ltd
Printed and bound in China

ISBN 978 1 474 71420 4
19 18 17 16 15
10 9 8 7 6 5 4 3 2 1

British Library Cataloguing in Publication Data
A full catalogue record for this book is available from the British Library.

Acknowledgements
We would like to thank the following for permission to reproduce photographs:
Capstone Press/Karon Dubke, 14, 15, 18, 19, 26, 27; iStockphoto: Christopher Fitcher, 23, Marc Dufresne, 13, Susan Chiang, 4, technotr, 6, Tsuji, 16, VisualCommunications, 7; Shutterstock: Africa Studio, 11, Chutima Chaochaiya, 10, Ensuper, 22, Faraways, 5, gorillaimages, 17, Izf, cover, Jeff Thrower, 9, manzrussali, 12, pirita, 8, Sailom, 21, steamroller_blues, 20, Torwaiphoto, 24, wavebreakmedia, 25

We would like to thank Pat O'Mahony for his help in the preparation of this book.

Every effort has been made to contact copyright holders of material reproduced in this book. Any omissions will be rectified in subsequent printings if notice is given to the publisher.

All the internet addresses (URLs) given in this book were valid at the time of going to press. However, due to the dynamic nature of the internet, some addresses may have changed, or sites may have changed or ceased to exist since publication. While the author and publisher regret any inconvenience this may cause readers, no responsibility for any such changes can be accepted by either the author or the publisher.

Contents

Some words are shown in bold, **like this**. You can find out what they mean by looking in the glossary.

What is a force?

A force is a **push** or a **pull**. If you push a door closed, or pull it open, you are using a force to make the door move. You use forces in everything you do, from pulling on your shoes to brushing your teeth.

This worker is using a trolley to move some boxes.

A crane uses a big force to lift a huge, heavy box off a ship.

People use machines to help them do things that need a lot of force.
Big machines such as bulldozers and trains can push and pull huge loads.

Effects of a force

Forces get things moving. A swimmer **pushes** off from the side of a swimming pool to start moving through the water.

A swimmer uses her feet to push against the side of the pool.

Cyclists make their bikes go faster by pushing the pedals harder and faster.

Forces also change how things move. A force can make something go faster or slower, or turn to the left or right. A cyclist uses the **pedals** and **brakes** to make the bicycle move faster or slower.

Changing direction

A force is needed to change direction. Turning the handlebar of a bicycle or scooter turns the front wheel. The rest of the scooter then follows the front wheel.

Turning the handlebar steers the scooter.

Hitting the ball with the bat makes the ball change direction.

In ball games, the ball changes direction many times. Footballers kick the ball from one player to another and try to kick it into the goal. Other games use bats or rackets to hit the ball.

Changing shape

Forces can make some things change shape. If you **push** something soft, you squash it. If you **pull** it, you can stretch it. You can bend a stick by pulling down the ends.

When you squeeze a rubber ball, it changes shape.

Modelling clay keeps the shape you make with it.

Modelling clay is easy to make into different shapes. You can push it and pull it into the shape of a person, an animal or anything you like.

Strength of forces

A strong force produces a bigger effect than a weaker one. If you kick a ball hard, it will go farther than if you tap it gently. A hard kick will also make it move faster.

A strong kick forces the ball to move fast and far.

How far the pebble goes depends on how much force is used to throw it.

The effect of a force also depends on how heavy the object is. You can throw a small pebble much farther than you can throw a large stone.

Rolling balls

You will need

✓ a bendy straw

✓ 3 different types of balls, such as a plastic ball, a table tennis ball and a marble

✓ chalk

✓ measuring tape

✓ paper and pencil

1 Chalk a spot on the floor and place one of the balls on it.

2 Put the end of the straw close to the ball and blow.

3 Measure how far the ball rolls.

4 Repeat with the other balls.

5 Which ball rolled farthest? Did any ball not move at all?

Check your results on page 28.

Friction

If you **push** a box across a table, the box will soon slow down and stop. The force that slows down the box is called **friction**. Friction is produced when one surface moves or tries to move across another surface.

Friction between the golf ball and the grass slows down the ball until it stops.

Skis slide easily because there is little friction between the skis and the snow.

Different **materials** produce different amounts of friction. Rough surfaces produce more friction than smooth ones.

Comparing surfaces

You will need:

✓ a board
✓ a box
✓ a toy car
✓ a measuring tape

✓ paper and pencil
✓ different surfaces, such as carpet, wood and concrete

1 Rest the board on the box to make a slope. Make a mark on the side of the board where it rests on the front of the box.

2 Place the car with its back wheels at the very top of the slope. Let the car go.

3 Measure how far the car travels from the bottom of the slope.

4 Repeat on other surfaces. Make sure that the mark on the side of the board is at the front of the box.

Check your results on page 28.

Using friction

It is hard to walk without the help of **friction**. Friction stops your feet slipping backwards, so that you can move forward. Friction is useful in other ways too.

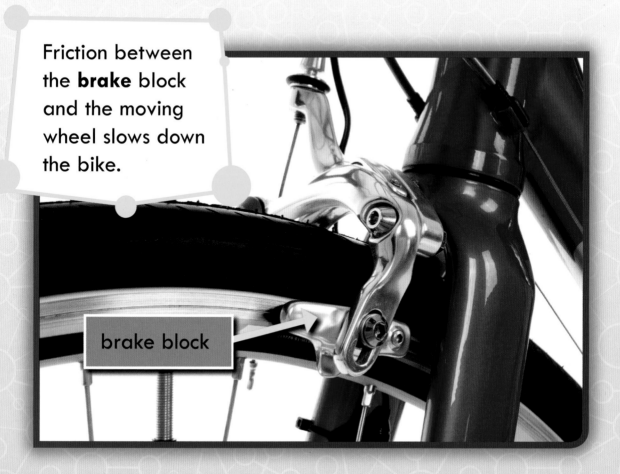

Friction between the **brake** block and the moving wheel slows down the bike.

brake block

The goalkeeper's gloves give extra friction to stop the ball slipping from his hands.

Some sportspeople wear special gloves to help them catch and grip a ball. The gloves are rough so they make lots of friction. The friction helps the player hold on to the ball.

Reducing friction

Sometimes **friction** stops things working smoothly. **Engines** include different parts that move as the engine works. Coating the moving parts with **oil** makes them work more smoothly.

Oil is poured into the oil pan and then pumped to the engine.

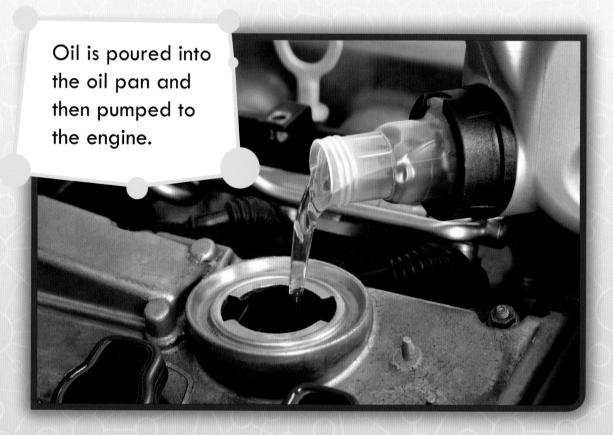

Skates slide smoothly across the ice because the ice is covered with a very thin layer of water.

Wet surfaces are more slippery than dry surfaces. This is because the water reduces friction between the surfaces.

Two or more forces

Two or more forces can act on something at the same time. One force can add to another force to make a bigger force. For example, you may help your friend to move a table.

Two people **push** together to move the broken-down car.

The side that pulls harder wins. Their force is bigger so they pull the other side over the line.

Different forces may work against each other. In a tug of war, two sides **pull** against each other. If the forces **balance** each other, the rope does not move.

Balancing forces

You will need
- ✓ a flat piece of wood
- ✓ a narrow wooden block
- ✓ 2 small plastic pots
- ✓ marbles

1 Make a seesaw by placing the wood over the block so that the wood is level.

2 Place a pot at each end of the wood and put 4 marbles in one pot. What happens?

3 Put 8 marbles in the other pot. What happens now?

4 What do you have to do to make the pots and marbles **balance**?

Check your results on page 28.

Experiment results
What happened?

Rolling balls (page 14)

You probably found that the lightest ball rolled the farthest and was easiest to blow. Was the marble too heavy to move?

Comparing surfaces (page 18)

You should have found that the car rolled farthest on the smoothest surface and least far on the roughest surface.

Balancing forces (page 26)

The end of the seesaw with the heavier weight (the most marbles) tips down. Putting the same number of marbles in each pot makes the seesaw **balance** again.

Quiz

1 You steer a scooter
   a by sliding your foot along the ground
   b by leaning to one side or the other
   c by turning the handlebar to turn the front wheel

2 Using a lot of force to kick a ball
   a makes it go farther and faster
   b makes it go faster but not farther
   c makes it go farther but not faster

3 If two forces act in the same direction
   a they produce a smaller force
   b they produce a bigger force
   c they balance

Turn to page 31 for the answers.

Glossary

balance when two equal forces cancel each other out

brake part of a vehicle that makes it slow down

engine machine that makes something move

friction a force produced when one surface moves or slides over another surface

material substance from which something is made. Wood, plastic, ice and concrete are examples of materials.

oil thick liquid found deep in the ground

pedal part of a bicycle that you turn to make the wheels turn

pull make something move towards you

push make something move away from you

Find out more

Books

Fizzing Physics (Science Crackers), Steve Parker (QED, 2012)

Forces and Magnets (Moving up with Science), Peter Riley (Franklin Watts, 2015)

Pushes and Pulls (Why it Works), Anna Claybourne (QED Publishing 2008)

Utterly Amazing Science, Robert Winston (Dorling Kindersley 2014)

Websites

www.bbc.co.uk/schools/scienceclips/ages/6_7/ forces_movement.shtml
Explore the effect of forces on a car and a truck in an onscreen activity.

www.hyperstaffs.info/work/physics/lall/1.htm
You can visit Jack's house, Sophie's house and The Park to click on different things and find out forces in each place.

Answers: 1c, 2a, 3b

Index